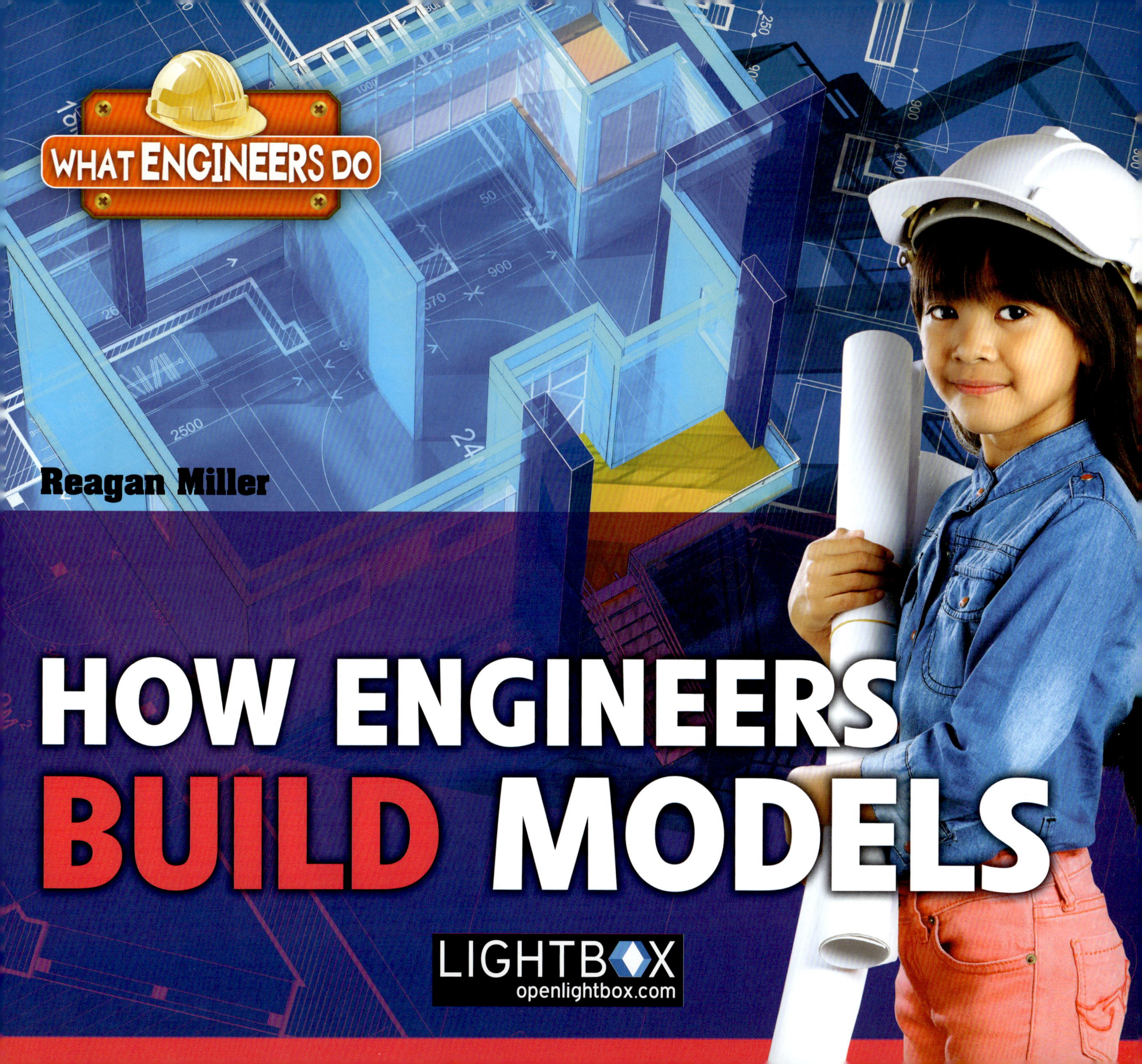

WHAT ENGINEERS DO

Reagan Miller

HOW ENGINEERS BUILD MODELS

LIGHTBOX
openlightbox.com

LIGHTBOX

Go to **www.openlightbox.com** and enter this book's unique code.

ACCESS CODE

LBXW8967

Lightbox is an all-inclusive digital solution for the teaching and learning of curriculum topics in an original, groundbreaking way. Lightbox is based on National Curriculum Standards.

OPTIMIZED FOR

- ✓ TABLETS
- ✓ WHITEBOARDS
- ✓ COMPUTERS
- ✓ AND MUCH MORE!

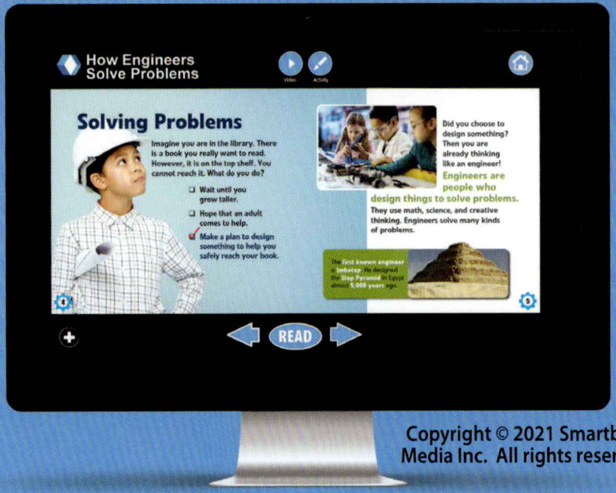

STANDARD FEATURES OF LIGHTBOX

AUDIO High-quality narration using text-to-speech system

VIDEOS Embedded high-definition video clips

ACTIVITIES Printable PDFs that can be emailed and graded

WEBLINKS Curated links to external, child-safe resources

SLIDESHOWS Pictorial overviews of key concepts

INTERACTIVE MAPS Interactive maps and aerial satellite imagery

QUIZZES Ten multiple choice questions that are automatically graded and emailed for teacher assessment

KEY WORDS Matching key concepts to their definitions

VIDEOS

WEBLINKS

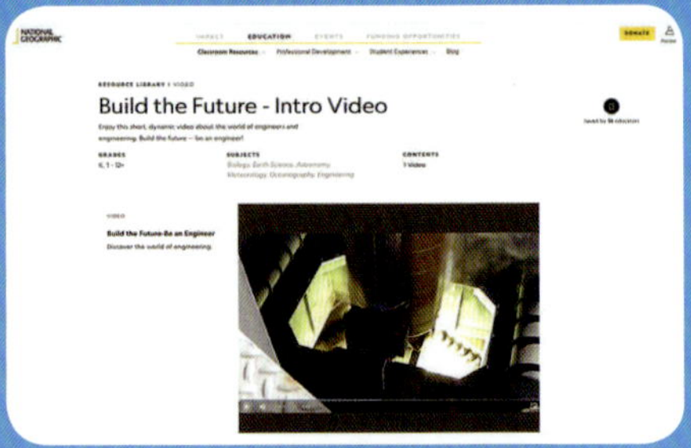

SLIDESHOWS

QUIZZES

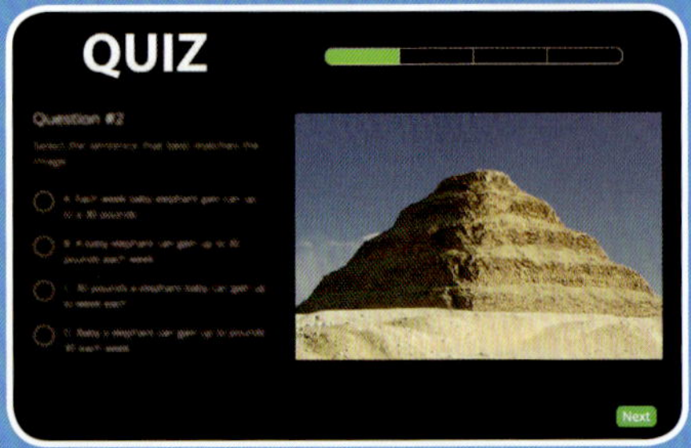

WHAT ENGINEERS DO

HOW ENGINEERS BUILD MODELS

Contents

Designing Our World

Look up. What do you see? If you are inside a building, you may see fans or lights. If you are out in a city, you will probably see skyscrapers. Have you ever wondered how these things were made? They were first created by engineers. **Engineers are the people who design many of the things in our world.**

The things engineers design are called technologies. **A technology is anything people make that solves a problem or meets a need.** Technology is all around us. For example, a car is a technology. It meets people's need to get from place to place quickly. An umbrella is also a technology. It solves the problem of getting wet when it is raining outside.

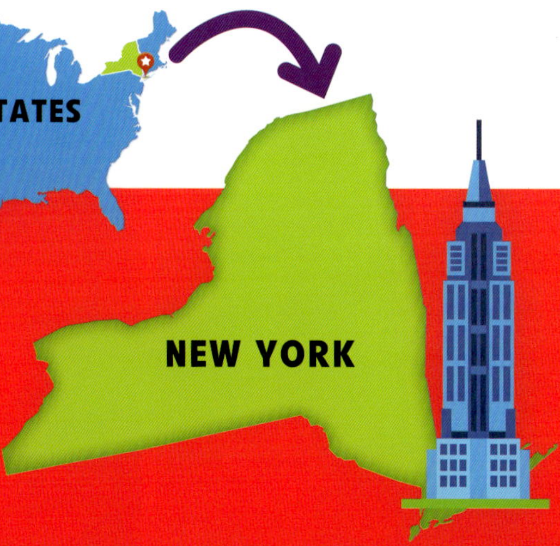

The **Empire State Building** in **New York City, New York**, is one of the most famous skyscrapers in the world.

Technologies Take Time

Engineers have important jobs. They use math, science, and creative thinking to design technologies. **A technology such as a bridge takes a long time to design.** Engineers must make sure it works well. It needs to be safe before people can use it.

Engineers often work together. They design technologies in groups. Working in groups lets engineers share different ideas.

Engineers spent more than **65 years** designing the **Golden Gate Bridge** in San Francisco, California.

What Is a Model?

Engineers communicate their ideas to others. One way to do this is by making models. **A model is a representation of a real object.** It shows how different parts of an object work together. A model can also show how something looks.

Have you ever seen a map of your school? What does it show? Maybe it tells you where the playground is. It may show the parking lot, too. **The map is a type of model.** It helps people understand what your school looks like.

Alike But Different

Models are not exactly like the things they represent. **Some models may not have all of the same parts or features as the real thing.** A toy car is a model of a real car. Like a real car, it has four tires. It can move forward and backward. The model is much smaller than a real car, however. It cannot move as fast.

Models are often used to show things such as wind turbines. A wind turbine is very large. It has many different parts. Building a real wind turbine would take a long time. It would be very expensive, too. **A model turbine takes less time and money to build.** It still shows how the different parts fit and work together.

Different Types of Models

Models have different forms. For example, a world map and a globe are both models of Earth. **A map is a flat model. It is two-dimensional.** Maps show length and width.

A globe is a solid object. It is three-dimensional. **Three-dimensional models have length, width, and height.** You can hold a three-dimensional model and look at it from above, below, and all sides.

Think like an engineer

A map is a two-dimensional model. A globe is a three-dimensional model. Give one example of another two-dimensional model and another three-dimensional model.

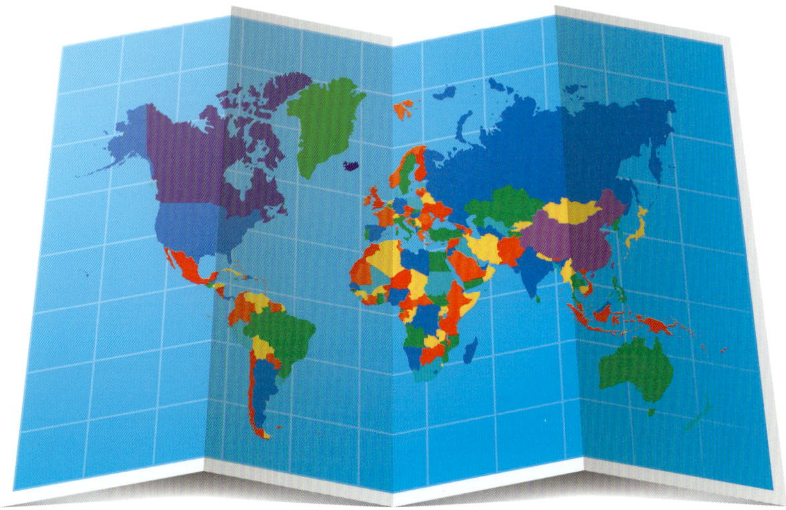

Diagrams and Blueprints

Some models are drawn on paper or made using a computer. **A diagram is a drawing of the parts of an object.** It shows how the object works. Diagrams have labels. Labels are words that name or describe different parts. They help other people understand the model better.

A blueprint is another kind of model. It is also a drawing. **Blueprints show the different parts of a building.** For example, a blueprint for a school shows where the classrooms will be built.

Think like an engineer

Here is a diagram of a backpack. The labels give information about its special features. Now draw a diagram of your favorite toy. What labels can you add to help others understand your model better?

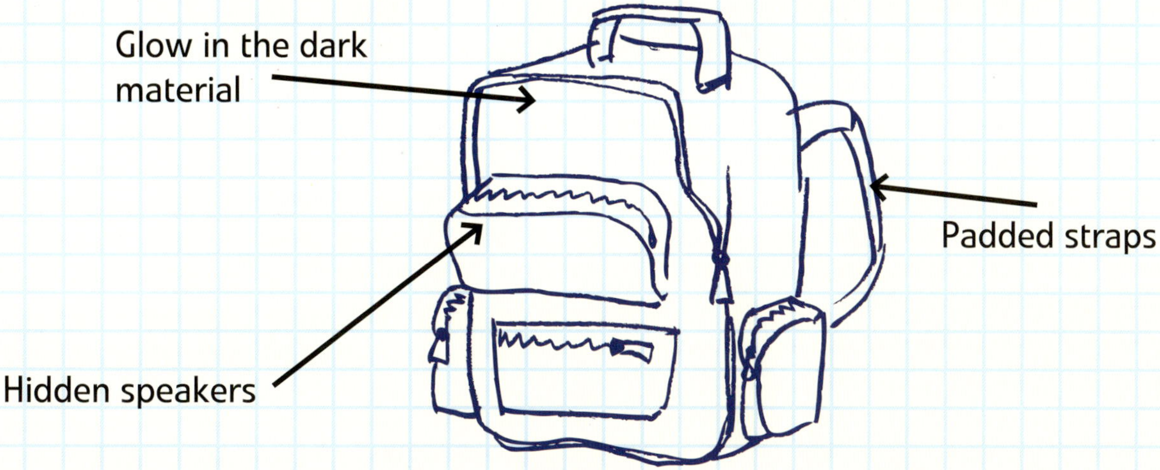

Models Are Helpful

Models are helpful in many ways. **Engineers use models to explain their designs.** Models help other people understand an idea. Some people may review models. They can give feedback, or suggestions. Feedback helps the engineer make the design better.

Models can be used to give directions. Engineers do not build the things they design.

They must communicate their idea to the people doing the building.

Models help engineers explain how something should be built.

Testing Models

Will a design work? Is it safe? To find out, engineers build and test models. Test results tell engineers what changes they need to make. **Testing models helps engineers improve their design.** For example, engineers test models of houses. They try to make houses stronger and safer.

Earthquakes happen in many areas of the world. They make the ground shake. Strong earthquakes can destroy houses. Shake tables move the same way as an earthquake. **Engineers test models of houses on shake tables.** This helps them see the damage a home would receive in an earthquake. Engineers try to design houses that will receive the least amount of damage from shaking. Tests show engineers which designs work best.

The **world's largest shake table** was built in **2005**. It is so large that most **real houses** could fit on top of it.

Choosing Materials

Materials are what objects are made of. Choosing materials is an important part of planning a model. **Different materials have different properties.** Properties describe how something looks, feels, or acts.

Some materials are better than others for making certain things. **Would you wear rain boots made of cardboard?** Of course not! Cardboard would let in water. Your feet would become wet. Rubber is a better material. Rubber is waterproof. It does not let water pass through.

ACTIVITY

Build Model Airplanes

In 1903, the Wright brothers made history. They became the first people to fly in an airplane. They spent more than four years building and testing thousands of different models.

Build your own model airplanes. Try using different kinds of paper. Change the shape of the wings. **Test your models.** Which design flies the farthest?

1 Fold a sheet of paper in half.

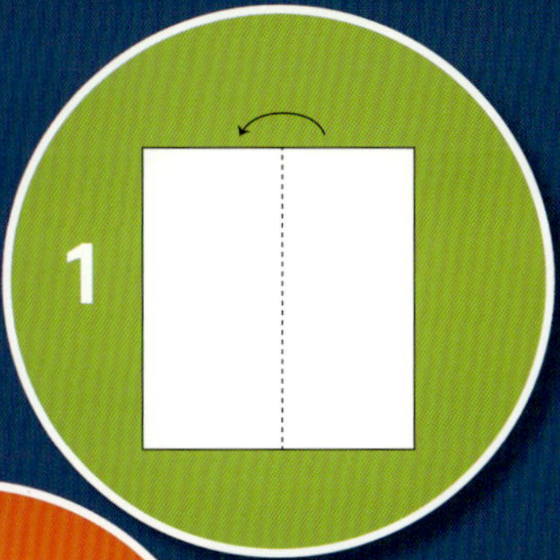

2 Fold the top left and top right corners down.

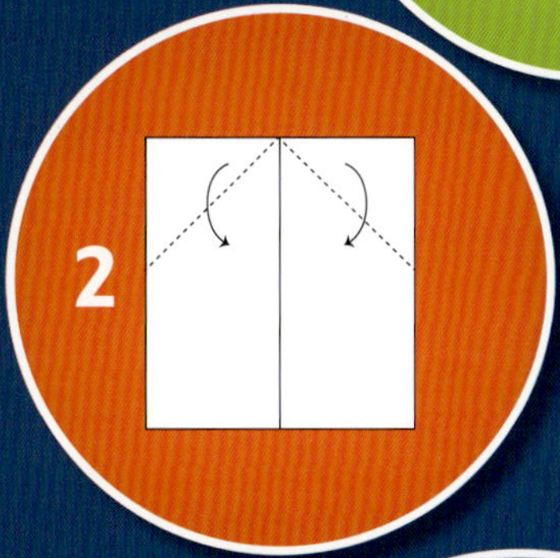

3 Fold the top left and top right corners again.

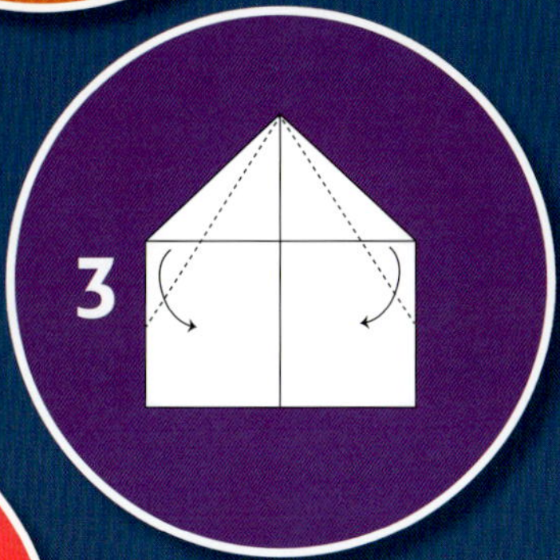

4 Fold the paper in half once more.

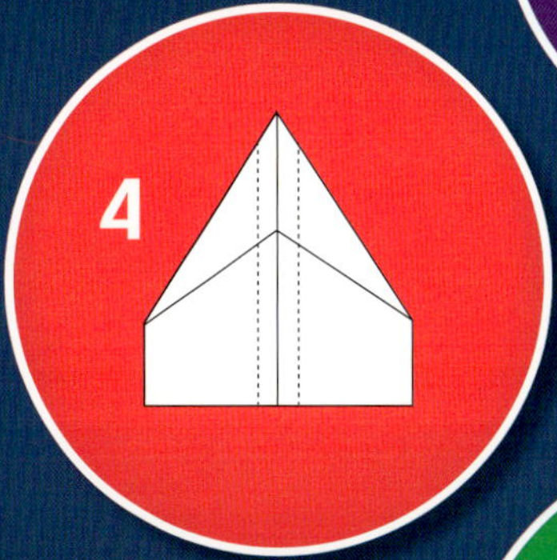

5 Fold down each side to make the wings.

Fly your model airplane!

KEY WORDS

Research has shown that as much as 65 percent of all written material published in English is made up of 300 words. These 300 words cannot be taught using pictures or learned by sounding them out. They must be recognized by sight. This book contains 138 common sight words to help young readers improve their reading fluency and comprehension. This book also teaches young readers several important content words, such as proper nouns. These words are paired with pictures to aid in learning and improve understanding.

Page	Sight Words First Appearance
4	a, are, by, city, do, first, have, how, if, in, lights, look, made, many, may, of, or, our, out, people, see, the, these, they, things, up, were, what, who, will, world, you
5	all, also, an, around, car, example, for, from, get, is, it, make, most, need, new, one, place, states, that, to, us, when
6	and, as, be, before, can, important, long, must, such, take, time, use, well, works
7	different, groups, ideas, lets, more, often, than, together, years
8	others, parts, shows, something, their, this, way
9	does, helps, like, school, tells, too, where, your
10	but, four, has, move, much, not, some
11	large, still, very, would
12	above, below, both, Earth, sides, three, two
13	another, give, think
14	kind, name, on, paper, words
15	about, add, here, its, now
17	should
18	changes, find, houses, try
19	could, home, same, so, them, was, which
21	feet, through, water

Page	Content Words First Appearance
4	buildings, engineers, fans, skyscrapers
5	Empire State Building, New York, New York City, problem, technologies, umbrella, United States
6	bridge, jobs, math, science
7	California, Golden Gate Bridge, San Francisco
8	models, object, representation
9	map, parking lot, playground
10	features, tires, toy
11	money, wind turbines
12	forms, globe, height, length, sizes, width
14	blueprints, classrooms, computer, diagrams, drawing, labels
15	backpack, information, material, speakers, straps
16	designs, feedback, suggestions
17	directions
18	results
19	damage, earthquakes, ground, shake tables, tests
20	properties
21	cardboard, rain boots, rubber

Published by Smartbook Media Inc.
14 Penn Plaza, 9th Floor New York, NY 10122
Website: www.openlightbox.com

Library of Congress Control Number: 2020936974

ISBN 978-1-5105-5417-7 (hardcover)
ISBN 978-1-5105-5418-4 (multi-user eBook)

Printed in Guangzhou, China
1 2 3 4 5 6 7 8 9 0 24 23 22 21 20

052020
110819

Project Coordinator: Priyanka Das
Designer: Jean Faye Marie Rodriguez

The publisher acknowledges Getty Images, iStock, and Shutterstock as the primary image suppliers for this title.

First published by Crabtree Publishing Company in 2014.